LAMAR COUNTY, GEORGIA

Pictorial History

SHANNA M. ENGLISH

Old Jail Museum and Archives

TURNER PUBLISHING COMPANY
NASHVILLE, TENNESSEE

www.turnerpublishing.com

Copyright © 2005, Turner Publishing Company and
Old Jail Museum and Archives
No part of this book may be reproduced or transmitted
in any form or by any means,
electronic or mechanical, including photocopying, recording,
or by any information storage and retrieval system,
without permission in writing from the publisher.

Turner Publishing Company Staff:
Randy Baumgardner, Editor
Peter Zuniga, Designer

Library of Congress Control No. 2005925626

ISBN: 978-1-68162-403-7

Limited Edition

0 9 8 7 6 5 4 3 2 1

Table of Contents

Foreword

In 1821, in a treaty by the United States of America and the Creek Indians, the area of present day Lamar County was surveyed for a land lottery. The whole area between the Ocmulgee River to the Flint River was awarded to fortunate drawers by land lots of 202 1/2 acres. In 1822, a portion of this was cut off to form Pike County, and this area included the towns of Barnesville and Milner. Barnesville was founded in 1826, and Milner was laid off in lots about 1845, after the Macon and Western Railroad was "put through" to Griffin in 1841. All of the communities and militia districts date from this early period of the 1820s through the 1840s.

In 1920, the state legislature voted to form a new county with the seat at Barnesville. Lamar County was chosen as the name in honor of the esteemed judge, Lucius Quintus Cincinnatus Lamar.

This pictorial history is intended to provide a glimpse into our economic and social development. The brief histories describing each community and militia district reflect the reasons for growth. The pictures document the images of people, places and things. The book is divided into communities and militia districts, because each community had, and still holds, their history close to their hearts. In many cases, the same families live in these communities today as descendants, and local heritage is richly guarded, even by "newcomers" to the area.

Creation of Lamar County

As early as 1869, during Reconstruction, the citizens of Barnesville began seeking a county of its own. Again in 1906, 1912 and 1916, they failed in their attempts to have a new county created, with Barnesville as the county seat.

In August 1920, local citizens once again called for a new county. Being defeated in the first vote in the state legislature, the committee came home on the train and held an emergency meeting with all citizens. It was made known that more money was needed to get the favorable vote in Atlanta. The citizens responded, and the committee returned to Atlanta on the morning train, with funds in hand; the second vote was favorable.

The act creating Lamar County was passed on August 19, 1920. The new county was comprised of the eastern portion of Pike County and the western portion of Monroe County, totaling 87 sq. miles. It was named for Lucius Quintus Cincinnatus Lamar, a well-known lawyer born in Putnam County in 1825. Barnesville, founded in 1826, was selected as the county seat. The new county began operating as a legal governmental entity as of January 1, 1921.

BIRDSEYE VIEW,
BARNESVILLE
GEORGIA.

CHAPTER ONE

Aldora Community

T he Aldora Community was created in late 1888, when the Barnesville Manufacturing Company built a cotton mill along the main railroad line, just west of Barnesville. There was a village built by the mill for its workers, who were known as "operatives."

The Town of Aldora was incorporated in 1906. The original village, located southwest of the mill, was torn down and some of the houses were moved to other locations. The present village is located southeast of the enlarged plant. Over the years, the mill evolved into tire cord production. The original plant has been expanded and is still in production today. The company is currently owned by a German concern.

A cemetery containing several graves of mill family members is located across from the mill along the railroad tracks. The coffins for the deceased mill workers were made in the mill.

There was a schoolhouse for grade school children, which is no longer standing. Aldora School, known lately as Graham Street School, was built during World War I. It is used today for the pre-school program.

Aldora Baptist Church and the Tabernacle Methodist Church were both active in the community. This wooden structure is maintained by Aldora, but not actively used.

Aldora Mills Picnic, 1950.

Curtis Clark climbs the pole at the Aldora Mills Picnic, 1950. Also pictured are Rene Jones, Poul Piper, Billy Watts, Gary Hearn, Ted Plymale, Cecil Turner, and Roy Bunn.

Potato sack racing at the Aldora Mills Picnic, 1950. Pictured are Tim Barlow, Pete Sutton, Roland Watts, Bobby Bunn, Poul Piper, Ted Plymale, Larry Hamby, Bobby Dingler.

Aldora Mills Picnic, 1950.

Aldora B-B-Q, 1950. Pictured are Rene Jones, Deland Renell, Gail Bunn, Peggy Sealock, Ted Plymale, Artie Edwards, Mildred Edwards, Edith Jones, Pasty Floyd, Silvia Piper, Phyliss Howard, and Gail Piper.

The Aldora Mills workforce, 1918.

Aldora School on Graham Street, 1960s.

Aldora Methodist Church.

Aldora Methodist Church Vacation Bible School, late 1940's.

Aldora Mills and village, 1970's.

CHAPTER TWO

Barnesville

The area known today as Barnesville was first visited by an Indian fighter named Jenks in 1825. He sold his interest in the land on which Barnesville was founded to Gideon Barnes, in 1826. Barnes built the first dwelling, the first inn and the first trading post. The settlement was originally called Barnes' Store.

In 1827, Barnesville was established as a post office and had its own stage line. In 1833, the road from Thomaston to Barnesville was cut by the Upson County Board of Roads. By 1841, the main railroad line from Macon had arrived. Most of the development during the period from 1830 to 1860 was brought on by the presence of the railroad. The rail depot was the center of the social and business community.

Sectionalism grew strong beginning in 1860 and continued until the close of the War Between the States in 1865. The economy during this period struggled and saw little growth. Progress began during the time known as Reconstruction. Lambdin & Pound founded the Barnesville News-Gazette in 1867. Summers & Smith began buggy production in 1866. Gordon Institute evolved in 1872 from the Barnesville Masonic Female Seminary.

People moved to town to work in the buggy industry and to educate their children at Gordon Institute. Workers located here to work as operatives in the cotton and knitting mills. The bustling town of 2,000 was home to approximately 40 businesses by the early 1880's. In October 1884, the town was devastated by a fire that destroyed 33 businesses and several dwellings.

The 1890s brought building codes by the City Council, a new fire house, a new Council room, the waterworks and the electric plant. But prosperity wouldn't last. Both banks failed in a general depression shortly after the turn of the century. Some of the cotton mills went into receivership, and firms had to reorganize.

With U.S. involvement in World War I came further economic struggles. The business climate was poor, and little new growth was realized. The optimism of the 1920's saw a surge in the housing industry locally. Many new dwellings were erected, resulting in vigorous activity in the building supply and contracting sector.

The economic climate of the Great Depression of the 1930's was stifling. People struggled to feed their families, and jobs were difficult to secure. Many local projects were completed through the Work Projects Administration. The courthouse, the county jail, the cannery and street paving of several streets were all part of this program, which created jobs locally.

Barnesville braced for the possibility of war again in the early 1940's. The local factories as well as individuals were affected by the rationing of certain goods and food stuffs. The composition of the work force began to change from male dominated to female participation when the men were called into military service. The war effort was supplied on the home front by female workers. After the end of the war, the work force remained a mixture of male and female. The woman was now part of the business world.

The peace after World War II was short-lived. The Korean Conflict in the early 1950s once again depleted the male force locally. Upon the veterans' return, V.A. loans facilitated a boon in the housing industry in Barnesville. The city laid-off the Veteran's Subdivision, and lots were sold to returning veterans. Community improvements included new playgrounds, a new swimming pool and a new maternity shelter. There was a sense of well-being and contentment in the community, as Gordon College celebrated its Centennial.

During the 1960s, the town enjoyed the status-quo until the Vietnam Conflict began to escalate. The anti-war sentiment eventually caused a decrease in the enrollment of military schools. Gordon Military College's enrollment decreased and the City decided to approach the Board of Regents with a plan to turn the operation of the school over to the University System. This proposal was accepted in 1972 and the school remained open. The institution was first chartered in 1852 and has remained in operation continually since then.

The birthday party of Louisa McCrary, held on Greenwood Street, 1910. Mrs. Lula Kendall Rogers, a famous teacher in Barnesville and Thomaston, is pictured at right holding the hand of Louisa. Among the other guests are Ben Hardy in the sailor suit; Mary Middlebrook, the baby held by the long-haired girl; Jessie Collier in the dark dress and bows; Elizabeth Hardy and Mary Hammond; and William and Charles Rogers.

A.M.E. Church in Barnesville (Bethel A.M.E. Church), 1895.

C.M.E. Church (White's Chapel) in Barnesville, located on Mill Street, 1895. This structure burned and was later replaced.

East Mt. Sinai Baptist Church on Washington and Jackson Streets in Barnesville. This building has been replaced with a new one.

West Mt. Sinai Baptist Church located on Zebulon Street in Barnesville. This building now has a new entrance and foyer.

Sanctuary of First Methodist Church, ca. 1911.

Advertising post card for First Baptist Church of Barnesville, on Zebulon Street, 1927.

Presbyterian Church in Barnesville, ca. 1927.

Sanctuary of First Baptist Church of Barnesville, ca. 1911.

*First Methodist Church
ca. 1927, before it burned
in 1939.*

*Pine View Baptist
Church, located at
Gordon & Collier Roads,
April 1967. The adult
women in the back row
include, from left: Mrs.
John L. Kennedy, Mrs.
May O'Neal, Mrs.
Joanne Hewitt. Also
pictured is Floyd Bates.*

A truck loaded with kudzu beside the Barnesville Depot, ca. 1930's.

Dixie Paper Shell Pecan Exchange, Inc., located in the original Summers Buggy Company factory on Forsyth Street.

Kudzu Advertising Postcard. Kudzu was cultivated near Barnesville for the mail order business of B.W. Middlebrooks, 1925.

Helena B. Cobb Institute at Washington Park, Barnesville, 1909.

Advertising postcard of Barnesville Court, 1950s.

First Baptist Church women, ca. 1920.

Carnegie Library, 1960's.

FUNERAL DIRECTORS AND EMBALMERS
Latest Addition Toward Rendering Beautiful Services
Ambulance Service Day & Night
MILL STREET   909   BARNESVILLE, G

Hunt's Funeral Home on Mill Street in Barnesville, later known as Hamm's Funeral Home, 1940's.

Jackson G. Smith in a Smith buggy made in Barnesville at "Cotton Carnival," 1900.

tern Auto Store located in the Old Gem Theatre, Doug & Agnes Lee owners until it closed, 1988.

Downtown Barnesville, east side of square, ca. 1962.

The Swatts Building. Tarver Woodall getting a shoe shine, with Roger Brown tipping his hat. The triangular block pictured, now known as Buffington's Building., was built right after the fire of 1884 by H.H. Swatts.

The Swatts Building., site of the US Post Office, drug store, barber shop, and lodge hall, 1895.

Wisebram's Department Store, with new modern aluminum front, 1960's.

Elijah Wisebram's Store on Main Street, 1920's.

East side of Main Street, 1975. Note the police booth in far center at traffic light.

Western Auto Store back entrance on Jackson Street (now Merchant's Way), 1975.

Gem Theatre, run by Wallace Smith, located next to the hardware store, 1930's.

The lobby of the Ritz Theatre on Forsyth Street, 1950's.

Gordon Cadets in front of the Ritz Theatre on Forsyth Street, 1945.

Lamar Electric Membership Corp. Building at the corner of College Drive and Taylor Street, 1949.

Akin's Feed & Seed on Market Street. Lamar Akin, proprietor, 1952.

Johnny Davis receives an award from a State 4-H worker in front of Akin's Feed & Seed Company, Market Street, 1950's.

Smith Shop, Inc. Furniture manufacturing at the old Smith Buggy Company on Zebulon Street, 1930's.

Smith Shop Baseball Team

Smith Shop, Inc. employees' picnic, 1940's.

Chief Tubby Ursery and Paul Smith of the Street Department emptying moonshine from a false bottom of a flatbed truck at Wilkes' Filling Station on College Drive.

Scott Riviere, Chief and Tubby Ursery, Patrolman, Barnesville Police Department, ca. 1940's.

Officer Tubby Ursery on patrol

Barnesville marshals E.R. Carswell, C.J. McDowell, and — Bankston, ca. 1906.

Chief Scott Riviere in the Barnesville Police Department's office on Jackson Street, now known as Merchant's Way, ca. 1940.

Police booth at the intersection of Main Street, Zebulon and Forsyth Streets, 1944.

Matthews Hotel, built right after the fire of 1884. The clock was moved to City Hall tower in 1932.

Roger Brown in Barnsville Hardware Company, 1990.

East side of Main Street, 1975.

First National Bank Building at the corner of Main & Zebulon Streets, late 1940. Note the Barnesville Fire Truck.

The Fire Department Christmas Parade in front of Wisebram's Department Store, 1950's.

Barnesville Fire Department at the Fire House on Main Street, 1960s.

The Nancy Hanks II train, which ran between Atlanta and Savannah, shown coming out of Underground Atlanta.

Barnesville Depot, 1916.

The Barnesville Depot at left and stock pens in the middle and on right, ca. 1890.

Stock yards behind the depot on the left in the rock building, ca. 1890's.

M. Burns, fourth from left; Mayor Cyrus Neuner, fourth from right; Chief Sam Taylor, third from right; and others, in front of the Nancy Hanks II train, 1946.

B. Lloyd's Pecan Products, located at B. Lloyd's Filling Station along the Dixie Highway on old Hwy. 41 near Milner, ca. 1940's.

B. Lloyd's "Nuts Did It" at the corner of Atlanta & Railroad Streets. The building was built as a knitting mill, then was used as Franklin Buggy Company, then Cherokee Casket Manufacturing Plant. A Chinese laundry operated in the west side of the basement level in the 1890s.

Shoe repair shop on Market Street, 1975.

Dr. William A. Wright, physician and pharmacist, mixing drugs in his drug store, 1870.

Ware's Upholstery & Pippin's Shoe Shop on Market Street, 1946. Employees pictured include: R.A. Ware, Mrs. R.A. Ware, Mrs. George Ryals, and W.T. Pippin, owner.

The swimming pool and golf course, 1970s. This site is now a parking lot and athletic fields for Gordon College.

Boyle's Good Food Restaurant, Ralph Boyles, owner, on the corner of Forsyth Street and College Drive, 1948.

Barnesville Planing Mill along the railroad track at the corner of Railroad & Mill Streets, 1960s.

Hamm's Funeral Home on Mill Street, 1968.

Tampa's Cafe when it was located on the east side of Main Street, where Pastime Grill is now located, 1950. The cafe was later moved to the NW corner of Main & Zebulon Streets.

Crossfield Ice Company, located on the south side of Market Street, 1955.

Dr. Rumble's funeral from his home on the corner of Lee & Forsyth Streets, 1913. The home was built in 1892.

Murphey Building, 1895. Built in 1884 on Zebulon Street across from the depot, the building is now the Armory Building.

Motley's Service Station, now the site of Barnesville Fire Department, 1947.

Carter's Mill, ca. 1970s.

Lamar Supply Company on Taylor Street. The site was built by James Porter and John Pennington in 1950s.

Drayman with load of cotton in front of Carter's Mill Nursery on Carletta Street, ca. 1935.

Lester Yarbrough's Drug Store, west side of Main Street, ca. 1950s.

Mangham's Drug Store on the corner of Main & Market Streets, ca. 1930s. Lori Mangham is on right.

Tommy's Food Mart on the corner of Main & Forsyth Streets, 1975.

Deraney's Store, 1975.

The corner of Market and the alley behind the Collier Building, ca. 1930s.

Keadle Hardware Store & Toyland at the corner of Main & Taylor Streets, 1975.

J.C. Collier Building at the corner of Main & Market Streets, originally the Lyon Building, built in 1884.

Holmes Hardware Store, located on the corner of Main & Taylor Streets, ca. 1910.

Roger's Grocery Store. From left: Cliff Wiggins, Harvey Burnettem, Sr., and James Rawls, Manager.

Crescent House Inn Motel and Restaurant, early 1970s.

Founder's Day Parade at Gordon Institute, in front of the Stafford Building, 1909.

Sullivan's Gin House on Taylor Street, ca. 1960s. Pictured are Jessie Monroe on right, and Joe Clements on left.

Mitchell's Feed & Seed on Taylor Street, now Two Brother's Cabinet Shop, next to Balamo Building Supply, 1964.

Fox Hunting near Barnesville, 1898.

Barnesville City Council at the Georgia Capitol in Atlanta, 1970. From left are: Tubby Ursery; Herman Andrews, Mayor; John Peavy; Ralph Barron; Joe Keadle; and J.R. Smith.

Country store built and operated by Berner Richardson on Third Street. This building was demolished in 2004.

Willie Hunt Chapter United Daughters of the Confederacy, 1946.

Colonial Stores Grocery (Red & White), located next to the Stafford Building parking lot. This building was demolished in the 1980's.

Packing house at Old Murphey Homeplace on Murphey Ave. Workers are packing peaches.

Stallings' Filling Station on Forsyth Street. Torn down in 1997, this is now the site of McDonald's Restaurant.

Restaurant and lodge hall on Mill Street, torn down in 1994.

Bush's Cafe on Mill Street, demolished for a Police Station in 1994.

Tree removal downtown, 1950's.

Bankston's Barber Shop on the west side of Main Street, 1975.

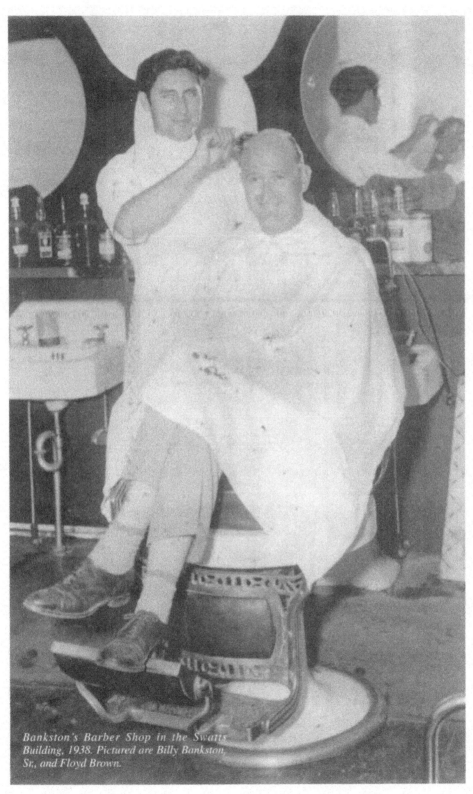

Bankston's Barber Shop in the Swatts Building, 1938. Pictured are Billy Bankston, Sr., and Floyd Brown.

Barnesville City Reservoir on Mill Street, 1895.

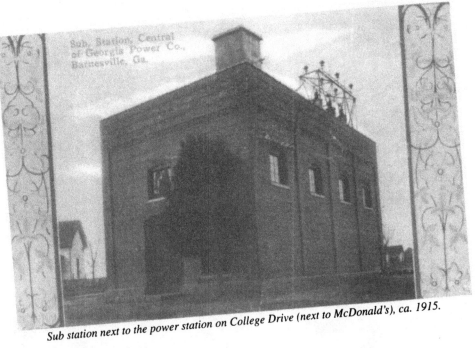

Sub station next to the power station on College Drive (next to McDonald's), ca. 1915.

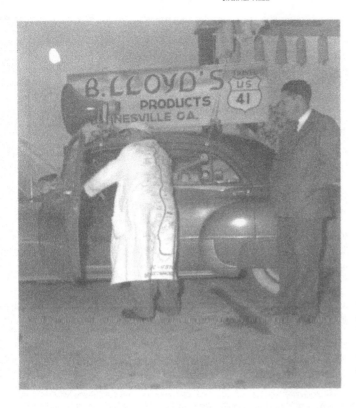

Dixie Highway Motorcade from Chicago to Miami, stopped at B. Lloyd's Service Station on Old Milner Road, two miles from Barnesville at Hwy. 41.

Karp Auto Supply, later Lamar Auto Supply Company. This building was later torn down for the expansion of Lamar Tire & Auto, located on College Drive.

First National Bank building, 1959.

Maternity Shelter & Health Department, 1952. Located on Gordon Road, it is now a dormitory for Gordon College.

Ambrose Means came to Barnesville with his "Wild West Show", 1912.

First National Bank Building at the corner of Main & Zebulon Streets, 1907.

Pontiac Dealership next to Sinclair Oil Company and Lamar Implement Company on College Drive, 1930s.

Frosty Palace counter during the 1950's. Located in the Stafford Building on Main Street.

Crescent House Motel & Restaurant, ca. 1950's.

M.W. Smith Building, soon after completion in 1905. It was built with a post office on the first floor, office space on the second floor and a lodge hall on the third floor. Superior Court was held on the third floor from 1921 until 1933, when the courthouse was completed.

Taxi drivers with their cabs, 1950's.

B.W. Middlebrooks Buidling on Forsyth Street, formerly the Summers Buggy Company, featuring Carriker's Filling Station, 1924.

Summers Buggy Factory, 1895.

Street scene on the east side of Main Street, 1916.

Summer Reading Program at Carnegie Library, 1957.

Carter's Mill Women's Basketball Team, 1949-50.

CHAPTER THREE

Chappell District

Lamar County was formed in 1921 from the eastern portion of Pike County and the western portion of Monroe County. The district court house at Unionville was closed and a new one was established in the Chappell community. This district court house was used to settle small claims, to pay taxes and to vote. It was named for A.H. Chappell who was for many years a State Representative. The community was settled long before it became an official district. It supported a general store, a blacksmith shop and a ginnery. Patillo School, Chappell School and Central School served the children of this community. The churches of the district include Pleasant Hill Methodist Episcopal Church and Rock Springs Congregational Methodist Church.

Chappell District School.

Chappell District Polling Place.

Interior of Chappell Mill where corn and wheat were ground into meal and flour.

L to R: A.H. Chappell and Dr. D.W. Pritchett.

Rock Springs Congregational Methodist Church, ca. 1950's.

Chappell Mill located in Chappell District.

CHAPTER FOUR

Goggansville

The community, first known as Goggans Station, was founded by the Goggans family in the early 1820's. It was later known as Goggansville and Goggans (Goggins). When the Macon and Western Railroad extended from Macon towards Griffin in 1841, Goggans Station became a stop on the main line. The depot was constructed across from the store building which still stands today at Goggansville. A pond nearby supplied water for the steam engines when they stopped at the station. The post office was in operation by 1875 and continued until 1920. Union Primitive Baptist Church was founded by pioneer settlers of this area and served as the religious and social center of the community.

In recent years the pioneer community of Goggansville has been included in the Johnstonville area by some local residents. However, Goggansville has its separate and distinct heritage from Johnstonville.

Goggansville Depot.

Union Primitive Church in Goggansville.

Store building at Goggansville.

CHAPTER FIVE

Johnstonville District

Johnstonville District, GMD 504, took its name from the Johnston family which settled the area. It was briefly the first county seat of the newly created Monroe County in 1821.

Early churches were Marvin Methodist Episcopal Church, Shiloh Baptist Church, Rocky Mount Methodist Church, Rehoboth C.M.E. Church and Bethel Baptist Church.

The post office was established at Johnstonville in 1839 and was operating until 1905 when it was discontinued and mail was delivered from Goggansville thereafter.

The former Johnstonville School, built in 1915, serves as a community meeting house. The brick country store is used solely for storage today.

Marvin United Methodist Church homecoming, 1952. Church located in the Johnstonville district.

Baptist Church in Johnstonville Community (Bethel Baptist)- photo taken in 1895. The structure has been replaced.

Marvin Methodist Church.

Rocky Mount Methodist Church in Johnstonville district.

Shiloh Baptist Church located at Lamar & Monroe Counties line on Highway 41.

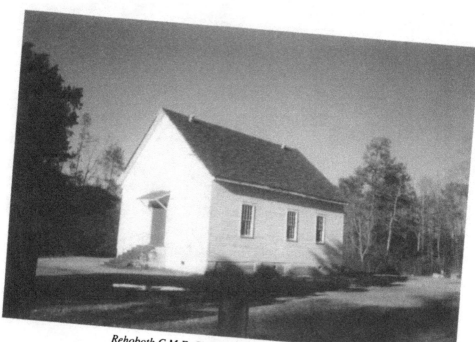

Rehoboth C.M.E. Church in Johnstonville District.

Store building at Johnstonville.

Johnstonville School in Johnstonville District, 1916.

CHAPTER SIX

Liberty Hill

Originally known as Van Buren, after President Van Buren in 1837, it was later named Davisville in 1841 and lastly as Liberty Hill since 1844.

Liberty Hill community had the distinction of being on the line dividing old Pike County and old Monroe County. It at one time had its own post office, a blacksmith shop, a tannery, a shoe making establishment, a mercantile business and a grist mill on Eady Creek.

Liberty Hill reached its peak about the time of the War Between the States. The stage line on the Alabama Road passed through this community. Liberty Primitive Baptist, County Line Primitive Baptist Church, Philadelphia Congregational Methodist Church, Hepzibah Missionary Baptist Church and Flint Hill Missionary Baptist Church were all active in the community at one time. Hepzibah and Flint Hill eventually merged to form Midway Baptist Church.

The mercantile business interests were sold in 1866 by T.S.M. Bloodworth to the Martins and later to L.F. Farley. The last proprietor was Dr. J.M.F. Barron whose activities were extensive and varied.

The old school house, the country store and post office are longer standing. The Community House remains the center of the civic and social activities of Liberty Hill.

Marilyn Barron English in front of the country store at Liberty Hill, ca. 1950's.

Pat Manry in front of gas pump at Liberty Hill country store and filling station, ca. 1950's.

Liberty Hill Church (formerly Primitive Baptist Church).

Liberty Hill Community house in the Liberty Hill community on HWY 36.

Shiloh Missionary Baptist Church.

New Hope Baptist Church in the Liberty Hill community at Eady Reek on HWY 36.

New Hope Missionary Baptist Church in Liberty Hill community-torn down and replaced with new structure. Picture taken in 1994.

New Hope Missionary Baptist Church field school- picture taken in 1994- no longer standing. Was located in the Liberty Hill Community on Eady Creek.

Liberty Hill Country Store and Filling Station, 1950's.

CHAPTER SEVEN

Milner District

This Georgia Militia District 540, was first known as Milner Station, named for Willis R. Milner. The town developed as a result of the railroad on the early 1840's. It obtained its charter in 1880. The district had three schools, a thriving business section and a post office.

Churches in this district include Spring Hill Missionary Baptist Church (later known as Greater Spring Hill), Mt. Sinai C.M.E. Church, Mt. Cavalry Baptist Church, Milner Methodist Church, Bethel Baptist Church and Milner Baptist Church.

The Women's Club House was torn down as was the major portion of the business section. The Milner School currently houses St. George's Episcopal School.

Greater Spring Hill Missionary Baptist Church located in Milner.

Mt. Sinai CME Church in Milner.

Confederate Cemetery in Milner, GA. Soldiers died in hospital there in 1864.

Milner School

Train car wreck of Swift meat bones, ca. 1950's.

Milner Community House, ca. 1950's.

Swint's Filling Station. Pictured: "Ink" W.K. Swint on bike and John Woodall standing, 1928.

Lamar County Marching Band with Director Dewaine T. Bell at Birch St. school in Milner, GA, 1973.

Class of 1942 Milner High school in old section that burned.

Pine Crest tourist Camp & Restaurant, ca. 1950's. Located on old Highway 41 (Milner Highway).

"Fats" & "Leans" Baseball teams from Milner, 1908.

Milner Methodist Church.

Milner Hardware Company, ca. 1900.

Milner Baptist Church, 1871.

Sanctuary of Milner Baptist Church which burned.

Swint's Pecans & Service station in Milner, ca. 1930's.

CHAPTER EIGHT

Piedmont District

This Georgia Militia District 1494 is the smallest district in the county. Big Potato Creek runs through this area. At one time the Southern Railroad extended to the Piedmont District. The depot as well as the country store and the gin house are no longer standing. A large portion of the business district was owned and operated by the Collier family.

On March 3rd, 1893, a disastrous cyclone devastated the entire district. Only three homes remained after the storm, the Colliers', Warthans' and Elliotts'. Several people lost their lives during the storm and as a result of the storm some days later.

Mt. Zion Baptist Church, Ebenezer Methodist Church, Midway CME Church and Mt. Pleasant Missionary Baptist Church are the cornerstones of the religious community in this district. All of these churches were founded by pioneer settlers and are still very active in the community today.

The Old Alabama Road runs through this district. This road was traveled by stage-coaches from Augusta, Georgia to Montgomery, Alabama.

Ebenezer School in Piedmont District, ca. 1900.

Zachariah Fryer/ C.C. Hightower plantation home located on Alabama Stagecoach Rd. in Piedmont District built, ca. 1850.

Dr. Blackburn's plantation on Piedmont Road in Piedmont District (located along Alabama Stagecoach Road) built, ca. 1830.

Ebenezer Methodist Church, located at the intersection of HWY 18 (Zebulon Rd.) & Highway 109 (Meansville Rd.).

Mt. Pleasant Missionary Baptist Church, Piedmont District.

Mt. Zion Baptist Church in Piedmont District.

Midway C.M.E. Church in Piedmont District along Thomaston R.R. Spur.

Ponderosa Inn Restaurant, located on HWY 36 West, ca. 1970.

.

CHAPTER NINE

Redbone District

This Georgia Militia District 539 is one of the oldest in the county. It was formerly located in Monroe County. Each church in the district had a field school next to its building.

The churches included Prospect Methodist, Ramah Primitive Baptist, Fredonia Congregational Methodist, Sardis Missionary Baptist, Sand Hill C.M.E. and Sugar Hill A.M.E.

Of two Rosenwald schools built in the county, the Sugar Hill building is still standing. The Redbone Community House has been and continues to be the meeting place for the various community activities.

Ramah School in Redbone District, 1916.

Prospect School in Redbone District, 1916.

Fredonia Congregational Methodist Church located at intersection of Brent Rd. & Fredonia Church Rd.

Prospect Methodist Church located on Brent Rd. in Redbone District.

Redbone Community House.

Ramah Primitive Baptist Church in Redbone District.

Sand Hill C.M.E. Church in Redbone District.

Sugar Hill C.M.E. Church in Redbone District.

Rosenwald School at Sugar Hill built in 1920's.

Summer Reading Program at Redbone District club house in 1957.

Annual conference at Fredonia Congregational Methodist Church in Redbone District, ca. 1900.

Crew running telephone lines in Redbone District, ca. 1918.

Lamar County farmers and County Agent, ca. 1950.

Ellen Sims Wideman, Cotton Picking Day, 1944.

"Cotton Picking day" at Rusk family farm near Barnesville in Redbone District, 1944. Stores and schools closed for the event to "get in" the cotton harvest while the young men were away at war.

Picnic at Prospect Church in Redbone District, 1902. Pictured L to R Front Row: Jim Abercrombie, Addie Mac Colquitt, Stewart Woodall, Malinda Graddick, W.W. Bankston, Lucy Bankston and Millard Bush. L to R Back Row: Hill Baggarly, Mamie Martin and Roy Sappington.

Sardis Missionary Baptist Church in Redbone District, established in 1841 as "Rocky Hill Nole".

CHAPTER TEN

Unionville District

This community, known as GMD 523, was a small community located on the Alabama Road, which saw dozens of stagecoaches a week traveling between Augusta and Montgomery.

The bustling community had a general store, a blacksmith shop, an academy, a common school, a cotton gin and a grist mill. There was a physician, a wagon manufacturer, a music teacher, a constable, a justice of the peace and a notary. The post office, established in 1833, received mail three times a week. It was discontinued in 1905. High Shoals Primitive Baptist Church and Unionville Methodist Church were located in the community. The schools included a field school next to High Shoals Church, Darden's School and Unionville School. The Monroe County Stockade was across from High Shoals Primitive Baptist Church. A district courthouse was built across from the general store. Small civil cases were tried here, taxes were paid here and voting was done here.

Unionville School in Unionville District, 1916.

Union Field School in Unionville Community. The only field school still standing in the county.

CHAPTER ELEVEN

Schools

Gordon College

Gordon Institute was founded in 1852 as the Barnesville Masonic Female Seminary by the Pinta Lodge No. 88. This academy evolved into Gordon Institute in 1872 and into Gordon Military School in 1897 when a military department was added on the eve of the Spanish American War. The school had an elementary department, a high school department and later a junior college department.

During the Vietnam Conflict, the concept of a military college became unpopular and the enrollment at Gordon Military College declined. The City of Barnesville offered the entire acreage and buildings to the University of Georgia Regents for $1. At their acceptance, the school became known as Gordon Junior College. The school began a two year Associate Degree Program in 1972, one hundred years after it became known as Gordon Institute.

Gordon Institute parade ca. 1910, in front of old Methodist Church (church burned in 1939).

Gordon Institute Founder's Day Parade, 1914.

Gordon Basketball Team, ca. 1920's.

Postcard, ca. 1890

Gordon Institute Library, ca. 1900.

Gordon Institute Football Team, 1916.

Gordon Institute, ca. 1890.

Gordon Institute located between Greenwood St. and Thomaston St., 1887.

Gordon Institute Class of 1903.

Play at Gordon Institute, ca. 1915.

*Gordon Institute Cadets,
ca. 1915.*

Gordon Institute Auditorium, 1925.

Gordon Military College

Gordon Military College alumni at a reunion looking at Gordon Cannons behind the Student Center, ca. 1985.

Parade on Forsyth Street, 1950's.

Nancy Chandler, Gordon College Majorette, ca. 1940's.

Gordon College Parade corner of Main & Market Streets, ca. 1960's.

Company C, Gordon Battalion, ca. 1922.

Gordon Military College Cadets on review at Gymnasium, ca. 1960's.

Anti- Drunk Driving parade for Gordon Military College Stafford Ave., ca. 1950's.

Gordon College Commencement.

Gordon College Centennial parade, 1952.

Gordon College Centennial parade, 1952.

Parade float sponsored by Dixie Paper Shell Pecan Exchange, Inc., ca. 1930's.

Turner Hall on Thomaston Street (now Lamar County Annex). Built in the 1920's as a dormitory for Gordon Cadets.

Gordon Cadets drilling at Summers field, 1927.

Bennie's Canteen at Gordon Military College, ca. 1950's.

L to R: Yarbrough, Callie Daniels, Rebecca Smith, Peggy Tyus, Loise Smith, Kathleen Kennedy, Jane Mangham, Doris Smith, Charlotte Moye, Carolyn Dickens, Sarah Abbott, Louise Lane and Kiki Burousas, 1938.

L to R: Louise Lane, Sarah Abbott, Carolyn Dickens, Yarbrough, Peggy Tyus, Louise Smith Jane Mangham, Kiki Burousas, Callie Daniels, Charlotte Moye, Rebecca Smith, Louise Smith and Kathleen Kennedy, 1938 at Gordon Institute.

Gordon Military Institute cadets drilling in front of Carnegie Library, 1917.

Gordon Military Institute "Central Georgia Club", 1918.

Gordon Military College Military Science Bldg., ca. 1960's.

Willis House Infirmary at Gordon Military College corner of Stafford Ave. & Gordon Rd.

Gordon Military College, 1943. Pictured L to R First Row: Donald Bebbe, Bobby Bush, Charles Ray, Marion Beavers, Richard Suggs Sappington, Bobby Chandler, Warren Proctor and Grady Dumas. L to R Back Row: Clayton English, Marvin Owen, Arthur (Smokey) Sykes, Kenneth L. King, Robert Sappington, Tommy Summers, Van Baker and Durwood Foster.

Gymnasium at Gordon College in 1952 Gordon Annual.

Gordon Military College Baseball team, 1938-39 year.

Sixth District A&M School

In 1906, the Georgia State Legislature created agricultural and mechanical schools in each congressional district. These schools would eventually evolve into technical schools. The school for the Sixth District was located in Barnesville. The City provided 300 acres and $50,000 worth of free light and water for five years.

The A&M School was closed in 1931 and reopened as the Georgia Industrial College. By 1933, this school was closed completely. At that point in time, Gordon Military College moved from its original campus between Thomaston St. and Greenwood St. to the A&M campus.

Sixth District A&M School, ca. 1918.

Students in the Forge at Sixth District A&M School, ca. 1920.

Sixth District A&M Basketball Team, 1929.

Sixth District A&M Baseball Team, 1929.

A&M Girls' Basketball Team, 1914. Congregational Methodist Church & Coca-Cola Bottling Plant in background on Greenwood Street.

Sixth District A&M School class of 1929.

Sixth District A&M School established in 1906. Later would become Gordon campus after 1933), picture ca. 1929.

Booker School

1960 Lamar County Bus Drivers L to R: Leonard Allen, John Bush, Sylvester Dees, John Henry Barnes, Eugene Perdue, Pierce Barkley, John Fletcher, Lewis Holloway and Corey Hugh.

Booker school built in 1957.

Booker High School football program, 1969.

1964 Booker High: #59 Oscar "Bill" Harvey, #74 Vernon Worthy and Coach Oscar Wimberly.

Barnesville High & Industrial School

Female faculty at Barnesville High and Industrial School on Mill Street, 1948.

Little Miss Elementary Contest Barnesville High and Industrial School on Mill Street, 1950-51.

Miss Barnesville Pageant at Barnesville High and Industrial School, 195-51. Pictured L To R: Mary Helen Watts, Estella Stephens, Queen Martha Mae Lee, Edna Maude Holloway and Agnes Brown.

Barnesville High and Industrial School Basketball team, 1950-51.

Booker High School Class of 1962.

L to R: William Fletcher and Charlie "Smity" Sutton, 1949 boys Region Championship.

Vacation Bible School at Barnesville High and Industrial School on Mill Street, 1950's.

CHAPTER TWELVE

Advertising Items

Advertising postcard for Smith Buggy Co., ca. 1900.

Advertising postcard, 1911.

Advertising postcard from the Chamber of Commerce, 1922.

HAVE YOU SOME PRINTING TO BE DONE?

Call your local printing office for your work. The Barnesville News-Gazette will do it efficiently and deliver it to you at reasonable prices.

We believe in doing a job right.

THE BARNESVILLE NEWS-GAZETTE

in Barnesville, Lamar's own paper

Phone 88

Advertising Ink Blotter for The Barnesville News-Gazette.

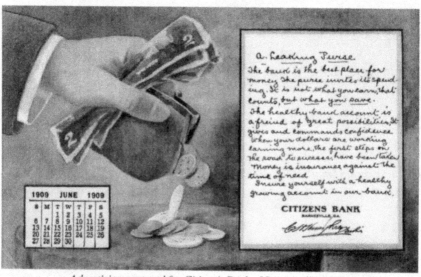

Advertising postcard for Citizen's Bank of Barnesville, 1909.

STRENGTH · PERMANENCE · STABILITY

JOHN R. COOK, Agent

Insurance & Bonds

PHONE NO. 166

BARNESVILLE, GA.

SOUTHERN DEPARTMENT
ATLANTA, GEORGIA

FIRE · AUTOMOBILE MARINE INSURANCE

Advertising Ink Blotter for John R. Cook, Agent Insurance & Bonds.

Advertising postcard for Smith Buggy & Sons, ca. 1890.

Advertising postcard for the Chamber of Commerce, 1909.

Summers & Murphey Buggy Co. Advertising postcard, 1878.

Advertising Ink Blotter for B. Lloyds Pecan Products.

Advertising Ink Blotter for B. Lloyd's Pecan Products.

W. R. BAIRD, BROKER
For Paper Shell Pecans

We sell direct to the consumer. Only the best varieties of Genuine Paper Shells are grown by us. Prices: 50, 60 and 75 cents per pound according to size. Delivered to you by Parcel Post.

Small and large orders solicited.

All orders will be given prompt, personal attention.

W. R. BAIRD, Broker,
Barnesville, Ga.

Advertising Ink Blotter for W.R. Baird, Broker.

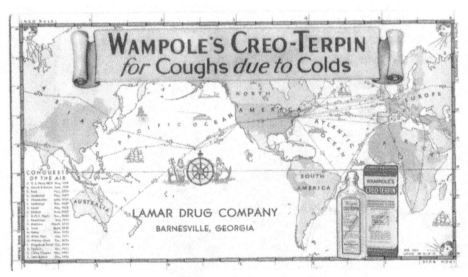

Advertising Ink Blotter for Lamar Drug Company.

HOLIDAY CHEER

PHONE 503

Fresh Flowers for All Occasions

BARNESVILLE FLORIST

815 Thomaston St.   ::   BARNESVILLE, GA.

DECEMBER 1949
SUN MON TUE WED THU FRI SAT
.. .. 1 2 3
4 5 6 7 8 9 10
11 12 13 14 15 16 17
18 19 20 21 22 23 24
25 26 27 28 29 30 31

39052 PRINTED BY BROWN & BIGELOW, ST. PAUL, MINN., U.S.A.

Advertising Ink Blotter for Barnesville Florist.

W. C. Jordan & Bro.,
Druggists,
Barnesville,   Ga.

Calendar Advertising top (located in the store of present day Carter's Dry store on Main Street), 1900.

JACKSON G. SMITH,

Barnesville Buggies.

The OLDEST in the SOUTH.

The BEST in the WORLD.

Advertising postcard for Smith Buggy Co., ca. 1890.

JACKSON G. SMITH,

BARNESVILLE BUGGIES

The OLDEST in the SOUTH.   The BEST in the WORLD.

Advertising postcard, ca. 1890.

CHAPTER THIRTEEN

Barnesville Blues

The Barnesville Blues was organized as Company D, 3rd Battalion, Georgia Volunteer Infantry of the State Militia in 1861, with Dr. George M. McDowell as their first Captain.

After training at Camp Stephenson in Griffin, the Blues encountered their first fighting at Cumberland Gap, Tennessee in February 1862. They continued to be engaged in fighting in Tennessee throughout 1862. Early in 1863, a Battalion of Sharp-shooters was organized and the company from Barnesville was chosen for their bravery and ability as marksmen. Ben Turner was appointed Captain of the Sharp-shooters. This unit was known as Company B, 4th Georgia Sharp-shooters. They were engaged in the Chickamauga campaign and the Atlanta campaign in Georgia. From the fall of 1864 through the spring of 1865, Company B, 4th Georgia was active in the Carolina campaign.

During the period of Reconstruction after the War Between the States, the unit was de-activated until 1874. The company was re-organized as the 5th Georgia Volunteers with E.J. Murphey as Captain. In 1894, he was succeed by J.F. Howard. With the advent of the Spanish-American War in 1898, the unit was changed to Company F, 2nd Georgia Volunteers. After the war, the unit under the command of Captain L. Swatts, the unit became Company G, 2nd Georgia Regiment, of the Georgia Militia.

In 1906, the Blues were sent to Atlanta to help quell the race riots. Days of violence occurred under mob rule before militia units from around the state brought back law and order.

In 1911, the Blues became part of the National Guard organization with Captain B. Franklin in command. In 1916 they were activated for duty on the Mexican Border under the leadership of Captain John M. Howard. Having been activated again in 1918 for duty in World War I, they became known as Company B, 1st Battalion, 121st Infantry, Georgia National Guard. After arriving in France in October of 1918, they were broken up and used as replacements in the 31st Dixie Division.

In 1922, the company was once again re-organized. During 1934 and 1935, they were called into service several times to quell disturbances in textile strikes, which occurred in several Georgia towns.

By 1940, they were activated for duty during World War II with Homer Sappington as their Captain. After the close of the war, they were re-organized again in 1946.

Barnesville Blues reunion on steps of Barnesville Hotel.

Barnesville Blues, 1928.

Capt. B.M. Turner, CO. B, 4th Georgia Sharp
Shooters (known as Barnesville Blues) & musicians
Allen G. Fambro & William T. Godard, Buglar,
1862.

William J. Goggans in Barnesville Blues
uniform, 1861.

Barnesville Blues- "Pussy Willow Squad", ca. 1920.

Barnesville Blues across from depot at Zebulon and Greenwood St., 1917.

Barnesville Blues in intersection of Main & Market Streets during the Spanish American war period, 1898.

Barnesville Blues in camp, ca. 1936.

Barnesville Blues, St. Simons. Island, Georgia.

Barnesville Blues in camp, ca. 1930's.

Barnesville Blues kitchen staff, 1941.

INDEX

Printed in the USA
CPSIA information can be obtained
at www.ICGtesting.com
JSHW021407120324
59073JS00004B/160